WILD WILD WORLD

FIDDLER CRABS

by Liza Jacobs

BLACKBIRCH®
PRESS

THOMSON
GALE

San Diego • Detroit • New York • San Francisco • Cleveland • New Haven, Conn. • Waterville, Maine • London • Munich

For more information, contact
The Gale Group, Inc.
27500 Drake Rd.
Farmington Hills, MI 48331-3535
Or you can visit our Internet site at http://www.gale.com

Photographs © 1991 by Chang Yi-Wen

Illustrations © 1991 by Cheng Xue-Fang

Cover photograph © Corbis

© 1991 by Chin-Chin Publications Ltd.

No. 274-1, Sec.1 Ho-Ping E. Rd., Taipei, Taiwan, R.O.C.
Tel: 886-2-2363-3486 Fax: 886-2-2363-6081

LIBRARY OF CONGRESS CATALOGING-IN-PUBLICATION DATA

Jacobs, Liza.
  Fiddler crabs / by Liza Jacobs.
    v. cm. -- (Wild wild world)
  Includes bibliographical references (p. 24).
  Contents: Environment -- Mating -- Dangers.
    ISBN 1-4103-0030-7 (hardback : alk. paper)
    1. Fiddler crabs--Juvenile literature. [1. Fiddler crabs. 2. Crabs.]
  I. Title. II. Series.

  QL444.M33J3 2003
  595.3'86--dc21

                                                    2003001467

Printed in Taiwan
10 9 8 7 6 5 4 3 2 1

Table of Contents

About Fiddler Crabs

Fiddler crabs are found on warm beaches in many parts of the world. There are many different kinds of fiddler crabs.

A crab has a soft body covered with a hard shell. Like all crabs, fiddler crabs have 10 legs. There are claws at the ends of the front two legs. Both of the claws on a female fiddler are small. But on a male fiddler crab, one of these claws is very big.

In fact, it is at least 4 times the size of its other claw. A male's large claw makes it easy to spot a fiddler crab on a beach.

Fiddler crabs use their legs to walk and dig. They walk sideways very fast across the sand. They can also dig holes quickly to hide from animals that eat them.

The Fiddler Crab Body

Fiddler crabs have eyes placed at the ends of long, thin stalks. This allows a fiddler crab to be partially hidden and still see what is going on around it. A fiddler crab can also wiggle its eye stalks to see in different directions at once.

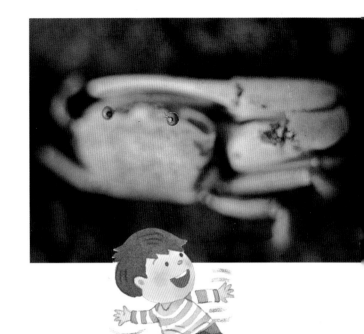

7

8

Claws

Male fiddler crabs use their big claw to communicate. They wave it to get the attention of other crabs. This is the crab's way of saying "Hello." Males can also make a rattling sound by waving their large claw. They make this sound to mark their territory. It is a "keep out" signal to unwanted visitors.

Unlike males, a female fiddler crab has two claws of equal size.

Burrows

Both male and female crabs dig burrows, or holes, in the wet sand. Some burrows are temporary—made quickly to stay out of danger. A fiddler crab's main burrow, however, is its home. It is about a half an inch wide and can go 3 feet down in the sand. Sometimes one burrow connects to others. Fiddler crabs also use their main burrows to escape attack, as well as avoid the hot sun and keep from drowning during high tide.

hen the tide
mes in, a
dler crab plugs
the entrance
le to its burrow
th mud to keep
rom flooding.
ough air is
pped inside
the crab to
eathe. Some
abs stay in their
rrows all
nter.

Food

At low tide, fiddler crabs come out of their burrows and search for food. They use their claws to eat.

The female crabs use both claws to pick up pieces of sand and mud. In their mouths, they separate the sand and mud from the edible bits of algae and other edible matter. The remaining sand and mud is left on the ground as little round pellets.

Mating

A male fiddler's big claw helps it attract a female mate. During a mating period, males build special breeding burrows in the sand. They wait outside their burrows for females to pass nearby. When they do, the males wave their large claw in the air.

If a female is interested, she comes near a male's burrow. The male continues to wave his claw and runs back and forth between the female and his burrow, encouraging her to enter.

When she does, the male follows her and the crabs mate. The female stays inside the burrow for 2 weeks. The mass of 100 to 200 eggs attached to her belly is called a sponge. The female leaves the burrow when she is ready to release her eggs into the water.

When the babies are born they do not look anything like crabs. As they grow, they their bodies become more rounded and they slowly take on the familiar crab shape.

Competing Males

A male fiddler crab also uses its large claw to defend its burrow from other crabs. And it uses it to scare away a male fiddler who is competing for the same female.

If one crab doesn't crawl away in fear, the two males will fight. They bob their bodies up and down. Each waves its large claw at the other. Things usually stay fairly calm, much like an arm wrestling match.

Losing a Claw

Sometimes, however, a fight between two males gets dangerous. If a male fiddler does lose a claw in a fight, the claw will slowly grow back. In the meantime, that crab will have a much harder time defending itself. It may not survive without its defenses.

Who Eats Crabs?

Fiddler crabs are eaten by many different animals, including water birds, fish, blue crabs, and raccoons.

A fiddler crab raises its claw to warn off an enemy.

People also eat crabs and gather them on the beach. Fiddlers live in large groups. This helps some crabs in their group escape being eaten.

A crab's hard shell also protects it from enemies. A fiddler crab is in the most danger when it molts, or twice a year. While it is growing a new shell, it is easier for an enemy to eat it. Fiddler crabs tend to stay hidden in their burrows during this time.

Unique Creatures

Fiddler crabs are found throughout the world. They come in a variety of sizes and colors. All fiddler crabs spend their lives on warm beaches. They are one of the many unique creatures that make our beaches a fascinating place to see nature at work.

For More Information

Nathan, Emma. *What Do You Call a Baby Crab?: And Other Baby Fish and Ocean Creatures.* San Diego, CA: Blackbirch Press, 1999.

Stefoff, Rebecca. *Crabs.* New York: Marshall Cavendish, 1998.

Glossary

burrow the home a crab digs in the sand

molt to shed

sponge a mass of fiddler crab eggs